THE LORD OF THE RINGS

THE TWO TOWERS

PHOTO GUIDE

"There is a union now between the two towers - Barad-dûr, fortress of the Dark Lord Sauron, and Orthanc, stronghold of the wizard Saruman."

First published in Great Britain by Collins in 2002

Collins is an imprint of HarperCollins*Publishers*
77-85 Fulham Palace Road,
Hammersmith, London W6 8JB

www.tolkien.co.uk

1 3 5 7 9 8 6 4 2

Text by David Brawn
Adapted from the screenplay by Fran Walsh, Philippa Boyens, Peter Jackson and Stephen Sinclair
Edited by Aisling FitzPatrick, Design by James Stevens, Production by Chris Wright

Photography: Pierre Vinet and Chris Coad
A catalogue record for this book is available from the British Library

ISBN 0 00 714372 9

Printed and bound in Belgium by Proost

THE LORD OF THE RINGS

THE TWO TOWERS

PHOTO GUIDE

Collins

An imprint of HarperCollinsPublishers

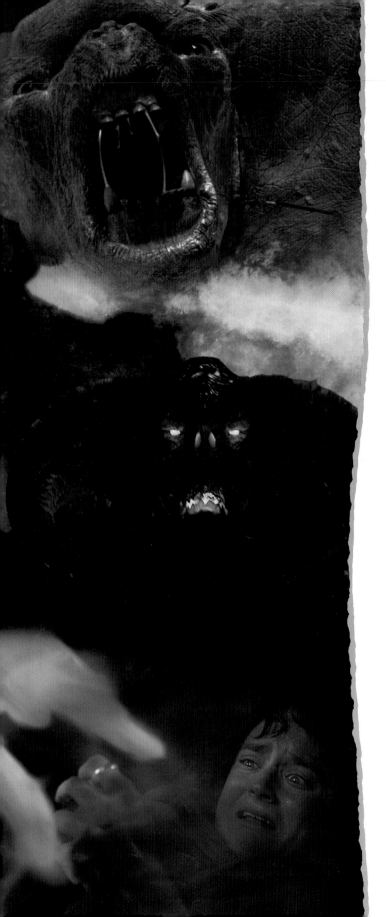

Frodo Baggins is troubled by nightmares. Since undertaking the mission to carry the One Ring back to the place it was made, Mount Doom in Mordor, the hobbit has faced many dangers. His friend Gandalf, the grey wizard, fell to certain death in the Mines of Moria while saving the rest of the Fellowship from the fiery Balrog; and now the traitorous Saruman has sent his army of Uruk-hai after them to retrieve the Ring. No longer knowing who to trust, Frodo breaks from the Fellowship to go on alone – alone, that is, except for his loyal companion, Samwise Gamgee.

"What is it, Mr Frodo?"

"Nothing. A dream."

"Mordor... the one place in Middle-earth we don't want to see any closer; and it's the one place we're trying to get to."

The journey is long and tiring. Sam is worried that they have come the wrong way, and Frodo is frustrated by their lack of speed. To make progress, they know they must get out of the hills and into the wasteland below.

But, someone is following them – someone who is waiting for an opportunity to seize the Ring...

"My preciousss..."

Separated from the others, Merry Brandybuck and Pippin Took are prisoners of Saruman's Uruk-hai warriors, who are now taking them back to their base at Isengard.

"I think we might have made a mistake leaving the Shire, Pippin."

Their captors are debating about why Saruman has ordered them to capture the two young hobbits.

"They have something… some Elvish weapon… the Master wants it for the war."

Pippin tells Merry what he has overheard.

"They think we have the Ring!"

"Shhhh – as soon as they find out we don't, we're dead!"

The three remaining members of the Fellowship of the Ring – Aragorn, Legolas and Gimli – desperately search for their captured friends for three days and nights. They discover Pippin's Elven brooch on the Plains of Rohan.

"They are alive!"

"Rohan…
home of the horse-lords."

The arrival of a hundred mighty horsemen, the Riders of Rohan, takes them by surprise. Their leader, Éomer, is Third Marshal of the Riddermark and nephew of King Théoden.

"What business does
an Elf, a Man,
and a Dwarf have
in the Riddermark?"

The Uruks' camp is attacked by Éomer's riders, and in the confusion Merry and Pippin escape. Fleeing into Fangorn Forest, the two hobbits are chased by the angry Grishnákh.

"Filthy little squeakers! I'm gonna cut maggot holes in your belly!"

An unexpected ally comes to their rescue.

"What are you?"

"I am an Ent. Treebeard, some call me."

Aragorn, Legolas and Gimli follow the hobbits' trail into the eerie Fangorn Forest. Suddenly, they glimpse an old man watching them through the trees.

"Saruman!" *"The White Wizard..."* *"No! It cannot be... Gandalf!"*

Standing before them is their friend and guide, Gandalf, restored to life.

"Far beneath the living earth... I fought him – the Balrog of Morgoth. Darkness took me... But it was not the end. The task was not done – I was sent back."

"He is the lord of all horses and has been a friend to me through many dangers."

The renewed Gandalf tells his friends that Merry and Pippin are safe, and that they must leave the forest. War is coming to Rohan and they are needed there. At the edge of the forest Gandalf summons his horse, Shadowfax.

Frodo and Sam finally catch the secretive figure who has been following them. It is Gollum, who once possessed the Ring and was corrupted by its power. He begs to serve Frodo, the *"Master of the Preciousss"*. Frodo accepts on one condition:

"You know the way to Mordor. You've been there before. Take us to the Black Gate."

Gollum leads the hobbits across a gloomy, bleak landscape, full of stagnant pools and withered reeds. But Sam doesn't trust him.

"It's a bog... he's led us into a swamp!"

As they continue their journey across the Marshes, Gollum tells them how his cousin, Déagol, found the Ring many years ago while they were out fishing. Gollum, or Sméagol as he was known then, wanted the Ring so much that he killed his cousin and stole it.

"Murderer they called us... and sent us away."

After committing this terrible crime, Gollum fled from his home and went to live in a cave under the Misty Mountains with only the Ring for company. There he grew wretched and miserable and full of self pity.

Reunited once more, Gandalf and his three companions gallop towards Edoras, the capital of Rohan.

"Meduseld, the Court of Edoras, where dwells Théoden, King of Rohan."

Approaching the Golden Hall, their way is blocked by the King's Guard.

"I cannot let you before the king so armed, Gandalf Greyhame, by order of Gríma Wormtongue."

"Would you part an old man from his walking stick?"

The king's niece, Éowyn, is mourning the death of her cousin, Théodred, who was fatally injured in battle against Saruman's Orcs.

Now she grows worried for the safety of her brother, Éomer.

Éowyn is pestered by the king's counsellor, the loathsome Gríma Wormtongue, who is captivated by her even though she despises him.

"Leave me alone, snake... Your words are poison."

"I understand. His passing is hard to accept – especially now that your brother has deserted you."

"Ever have you been the herald of woe. Why should I welcome you, Gandalf Stormcrow?"

Gandalf is taken before King Théoden and is shocked at how old the monarch has grown since they last met. He senses Saruman's influence over the king…

"Too long have you sat in the shadows. Harken to me! I release you from this spell!"

Gríma Wormtongue realises what is happening but reacts too late.

*"His staff!
I told you to take
the wizard's staff!"*

Released from Saruman's power, Théoden comes to his senses, regaining his old strength. Wormtongue is revealed to be a traitor, and the king throws him out of the palace.

"Ever his whispering was in your ears... poisoning your thoughts."

"Banishment is too good for you."

Saruman is furious that Gandalf has released King Théoden from his spell. Now more drastic actions are required to conquer the kingdom of Rohan.

Arming a rabble of five hundred Dunlendings and Wild Men, savages who live in the hills around Rohan, Saruman sends them on a rampage of chaos and destruction.

"Take back the lands they stole from you. Burn every village!"

"This is but a taste of the terror Saruman will unleash..."

Gandalf counsels King Théoden to send his troops to fight Saruman's army and draw them away from the women and children. The king decides to evacuate the city and take all his people to the safety of the mighty fortress of Helm's Deep.

Aragorn helps to oversee the departure of the last of the horses. Brego, the battle-worn steed of the dead prince, Théodred, is too distressed to carry another rider.

"Turn this fellow free. He has seen enough of war."

Gollum leads Frodo and Sam to the Black Gates of Mordor which span a deep valley between the grim, grey mountains. They are guarded by fierce Orc sentries.

"Master says bring usss to the Gatesss, so good Sméagol does."

A long column of fearsome-looking Easterlings march past Sam and Frodo and through the great iron gates into Mordor.

"Well that's it, then. We can't get in there."

Gríma Wormtongue returns to his true master. He tells Saruman that King Théoden's instinct will be to make for Helm's Deep. Saruman decides to send his Orcs to attack the refugees.

"Théoden made two mistakes.
First he trusted you, then he let you live."

At the City of the Trees, Elrond calls a council of the Elves. He believes that they should help in the struggle against Sauron, but not everyone agrees.

"The Rings of the Elf Lords were not made as weapons of war or conquest. They cannot come to the aid of Men."

"The alliance between Men and Elves is over."

Later, Elrond confronts his daughter Arwen about her decision to stay behind with Aragorn. By pledging her love to a mortal man, she must accept that she will grow old and die with him while her people remain young for ever. Elrond thinks she has made the wrong choice.

"There is nothing here for you, only death."

"Wargs!!!"

As the refugees and soldiers pass through the mountains, they are ambushed by Orcs riding giant wolf-beasts. They break ranks to engage the legion of snarling Wargs which attack them, and Aragorn becomes locked in a deadly battle with Sharku.

Reaching the woods of Ithilien, Frodo and Sam run into a party of Gondorian Rangers, who mistake them for Orc spies. They are blindfolded and taken to their hideaway, Henneth Annûn.

The Rangers discover the nature of Frodo's mission. Hearing that Boromir was one of the Fellowship, the Rangers' leader, Faramir, has shocking news…

"You were a friend of Boromir?
It would grieve you, then, to learn that he is dead?"

Faramir reveals that he is Boromir's brother and the son of Lord Denethor, the Steward of Gondor. Learning of the One Ring, he vows to take the Ring to Gondor, and complete Boromir's mission.

Treebeard carries Merry and Pippin deep into the forest. They reach the Entmoot, a gathering of many different tree-people, and wait patiently while the spirits of the forest discuss their fate.

"It's been going on for hours."

"They must have decided something by now."

"Decided? We've only just finished saying Good Morning!*"*

Merry and Pippin's appeal to the Ents to help in the fight against the evil of Isengard stirs them up, and they agree to march to Saruman's lair.

"It is likely, my friends, that we go to our doom: the last march of the Ents..."

The refugees and Rohan soldiers finally reach the ancient fortress of Helm's Deep. They gather in the Hornburg courtyard.

As Legolas and Gimli gallop through the gates, King Théoden tells Éowyn how they were ambushed and that many of their number were killed.

"Lord Aragorn – where is he?"

"He fell defending the retreat."

Having fallen in battle with Sharku, Aragorn is barely alive. As he struggles to get up, an unexpected champion comes to his aid.

"Brego...?"

Brought safely to Helm's Deep by Brego, Aragorn has urgent news for King Théoden. He has seen thousands of Uruk-hai marching towards the fortress.

"All Isengard has emptied… Ten thousand strong at least. It is an army bred for one purpose – to destroy the world of Men."

Legolas is worried: the defenders are frightened, and he fears three hundred of them cannot hold out against an army of ten thousand Uruk-hai. He feels betrayed by his own people and believes that the Elves should not have left the Men to stand alone.

The Uruks reach Helm's Deep and the great battle begins!

The Rangers reach Osgiliath, once one of the greatest cities in all of Gondor, but now in ruins after years of war. Faramir intends to take Frodo with him to the city of Minas Tirith and use the Ring in their struggle against Sauron. Sam pleads with him:

"The Ring will not save Gondor."

Faramir finally sees the evil in the Ring and realises that it is impossible to use it for good. He is persuaded to let Frodo, Sam and Gollum continue their journey to Mordor, and leads them to the old sewers where they can pass underneath the patrolling Orcs.

"Go, Frodo, go with the good will of all Men."

Merry and Pippin arrive at Isengard with the marching Ents. From his tower, Saruman watches as the massive tree-people break down the walls around his stronghold.

"There is a wizard to manage here... locked in his tower!"

Meanwhile, weary from the battle of Helm's Deep, Gandalf the White warns his friends that they have not seen the last of the Orcs and their kind.

"Sauron's wrath will be terrible and his retribution swift.
The battle for Helm's Deep is over. The battle for
Middle-earth is about to begin."

"All our hopes now lie with two little hobbits…
somewhere in the wilderness."